May

K. C. KELLEY • BOB OSTROM

The Child's World

Published by The Child's World®
1980 Lookout Drive • Mankato, MN 56003-1705
800-599-READ • www.childsworld.com

Acknowledgments
The Child's World®: Mary Berendes, Publishing Director
The Design Lab: Design
Jody Jensen Shaffer: Editing and Fact-Checking

Photo credits
© beltsazar/Shutterstock.com: 22 (top); Boykung/Shutterstock.com: 6; Brent Hofacker/Shutterstock.com: 10; Featureflash/Shutterstock.com: 23 (top); FrankyDeMeyer/iStock.com:12 (bottom); Helga Esteb/Shutterstock.com: 19 (bottom); Library of Congress: 20 (top); Lori Sparkia/Shutterstock.com: 13 (top); Marie C Fields/Shutterstock.com: 12 (top); Monkey Business Images/Shutterstock.com: cover, 1, 5, 11 (both-); NASA: 20 (center); National Archives: 20 (bottom); ruvanboshoff/iStock.com: 19 (top); s_bukley/Shutterstock.com: 22 (bottom); thatsmymop/Shutterstock.com: 23 (middle); Volosina/Shutterstock.com: 13 (bottom); www.NASA.gov: 18; wynnter/iStock.com: 23 (bottom)

ISBN 9781626873704
LCCN 2014930709

Printed in the United States of America
Mankato, MN
October, 2014
PA02250

ABOUT THE AUTHOR

K.C. Kelley has written dozens of books for young readers on everything from sports to nature to history. He was born in January, loves April because that's when baseball begins, and loves to take vacations in August!

ABOUT THE ILLUSTRATOR

Bob Ostrom has been illustrating books for twenty years. A graduate of the New England School of Art & Design at Suffolk University, Bob has worked for such companies as Disney, Nickelodeon, and Cartoon Network. He lives in North Carolina with his wife and three children.

Contents

WELCOME TO MAY!

Spring is in full swing in May! The weather is warming up, and the flowers are blooming. Around the world, May Day is a huge holiday. In America, May is packed with holidays all month long!

May FACT BOX

Order: Fifth

Days: 31

STAR WARS DAY

Can you figure out why May 4 is now called Star Wars Day? If you know the story, the heroes in the movie use "The Force." People wish each other well by saying, "May the Force be with you." May the Fourth...now do you get it?

HOW DID MAY GET ITS NAME?

Most experts think May is for Mom! That is, Maia, the mother of the Roman god Hermes.

Birthstone

Each month has a stone linked to it. People who have birthdays in that month call it their birthstone. For May, it's the green emerald.

MAY AROUND THE WORLD

Here is the name of this month in other languages.

Chinese	Wŭ yuè
Dutch	Mei
English	May
French	Mai
German	der Mai
Italian	Maggio
Japanese	Gogatsu
Spanish	Mayo
Swahili	Mei

MAY AROUND THE WORLD

May 5 is a holiday in Mexico called *Cinco de Mayo* (which means "May 5" in Spanish). This holiday celebrates a battle Mexico won in 1862. Many Americans have started celebrating the holiday, too. Los Angeles, Chicago, and Denver all have big parties and parades.

BIG MAY HOLIDAYS

May Day, May 1

In much of the world, May Day is when spring begins. May Day is a very big event in Europe, and some places in the U.S. have parties. The Maypole is part of some of those parties. People dance in a circle around the pole, winding ribbons round and round it. In England, people choose a May Queen at their events.

MAYDAY!

If a sailor is in trouble, he calls, "Mayday! Mayday! Mayday!" over the radio. He's not calling for the holiday. He's calling for help! This mayday is from the French word *m'aider* (MEH-dahr). That means "Help me!"

8

Mothers' Day, Second Sunday

Mother's Day is always the second Sunday in May. It became an official U.S. holiday in 1914. A woman named Anna Jarvis came up with the idea. It's a way to say thanks to all of our moms!

Memorial Day, Last Monday

The last Monday in May is Memorial Day. This is another day we say thanks. A memorial remembers someone who has died. On Memorial Day, Americans remember the men and women who died in the military.

KENTUCKY DERBY

The first Saturday in May is Derby Day. The Kentucky Derby is held each year on that day. America's oldest horse race was first held in 1875! The race takes place at Churchill Downs in Louisville, Kentucky. Fans pack the stands in their fancy hats! Millions more watch on TV. The race is nicknamed "The Run for the Roses." The winning horse gets a blanket made of roses!

FUN MAY DAYS

May has more ways to celebrate than just picking flowers on May Day! Here are some of the unusual holidays you can enjoy in May:

May 5

National Hoagie Day

FIRST OR SECOND TUESDAY

National Teacher Day

May 8

No Socks Day

May 12

International Nurses Day

May 15

National Chocolate Chip Day

May 16

Love a Tree Day

May 18

International Museum Day

May 25

National
Tap Dance Day

May 31

National
Macaroon Day

MAY WEEKS AND MONTHS

Holidays don't just mean days…you can celebrate for a week, too! You can also have fun all month long. Find out more about these ways to enjoy May!

MAY WEEKS

National Wildflower Week: Wildflowers are wild—they're not planted by people. The colorful blossoms decorate fields all over the place. This week, look for some near you!

National Police Week: A big meeting of police officers is held, often in Washington DC. They honor those who gave their lives helping others. They also look for new ways to serve the people.

National Nurses Week: Why honor nurses in May? We should honor them all the time! But this time is special. Famed nurse Florence Nightingale was born on May 12.

MAY MONTHS

National Barbecue Month: Memorial Day (page 9) kicks off summer. Barbecues are a part of many Memorial Day picnics. This month, start planning your holiday feast early!

National Foster Care Month: Some children do not have a home or family of their own. Volunteers and government workers help these foster children. They find safe homes and loving families to help these kids grow up. This month, we honor the kids and those helpful adults.

National Bike Month: Celebrate life on two wheels! This month, climb on a bike and take a spin. Many people ride to work or school this month. It's fun and it's good exercise!

MAY AROUND THE WORLD

Countries around the world celebrate in May. Find these countries on the map. Then read about how people there have fun in May!

Monday Before May 25

Victoria Day, Canada
Canada was a colony of Great Britain for centuries. This holiday looks back on one of Britain's rulers, Queen Victoria.

A TRIPLE TREAT

South Korea has three linked holidays. Each honors a group in their country. The first is Children's Day (May 5). Many families hold picnics that day. May 8 is Parents' Day, when children thank mom and dad! Finally, May 15 is Teachers' Day.

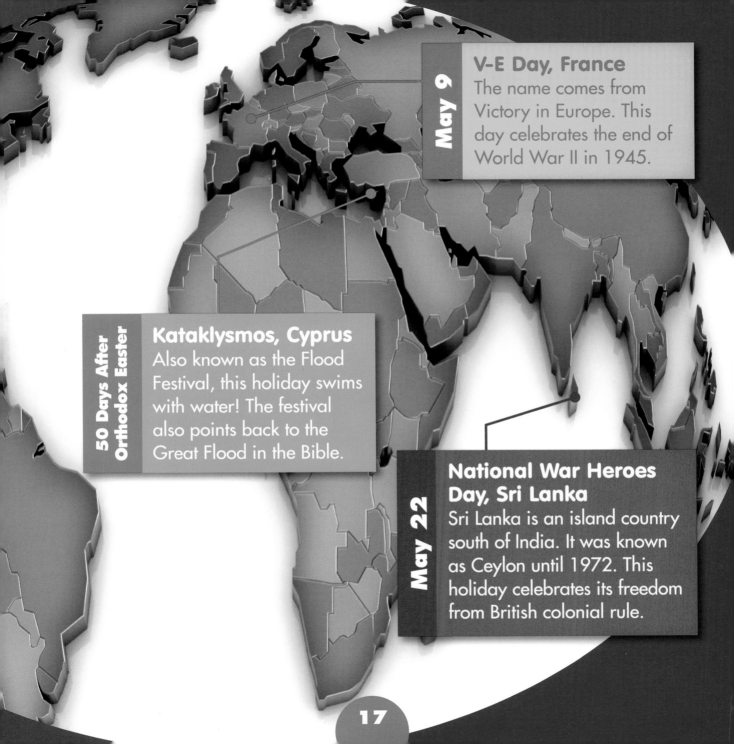

May 9

V-E Day, France
The name comes from Victory in Europe. This day celebrates the end of World War II in 1945.

50 Days After Orthodox Easter

Kataklysmos, Cyprus
Also known as the Flood Festival, this holiday swims with water! The festival also points back to the Great Flood in the Bible.

May 22

National War Heroes Day, Sri Lanka
Sri Lanka is an island country south of India. It was known as Ceylon until 1972. This holiday celebrates its freedom from British colonial rule.

17

MAY IN HISTORY

May 1, 1707

Scotland joined with Great Britain and Wales to form the United Kingdom.

May 5, 1961

In 1961, astronaut Alan Shepard flew into space. He was only up for 15 minutes, but he was the first American in space!

WORLD RED CROSS DAY

For more than 150 years, the Red Cross has been on the scene to help. Storms, earthquakes, wars, floods—if there's trouble, the Red Cross is there. Volunteers around the world set May 8 aside to remember Henry Dunant, who founded the Red Cross. Cool fact: in some European countries, the groups are called Red Crescent.

May 10, 1869

At a ceremony in Utah, workers finished building a railroad across America.

May 10, 1994

In South Africa, Nelson Mandela was made president. He was the first black person to lead that nation.

May 14, 1804

A party of explorers left St. Louis to explore the west. Led by Lewis and Clark, they reached Oregon almost two years later.

May 16, 1929

The Oscars were first given out in Hollywood. They are also known as the Academy Awards.

May 21, 1927

Charles Lindbergh landed his airplane in France. He had left from New York 33 hours later. He was the first person to fly across the Atlantic Ocean.

May 21, 1932

Amelia Earhart made the same trip in 13 hours. She was the first woman to cross the Atlantic.

May 22, 1972

President Richard Nixon (far right) visited the Soviet Union. He was the first president to make this trip to a country that was then an enemy.

NEW STATES!

Four states first joined the United States in May. Do you live in any of these? If you do, then make sure and say, "Happy Birthday!" to your state.

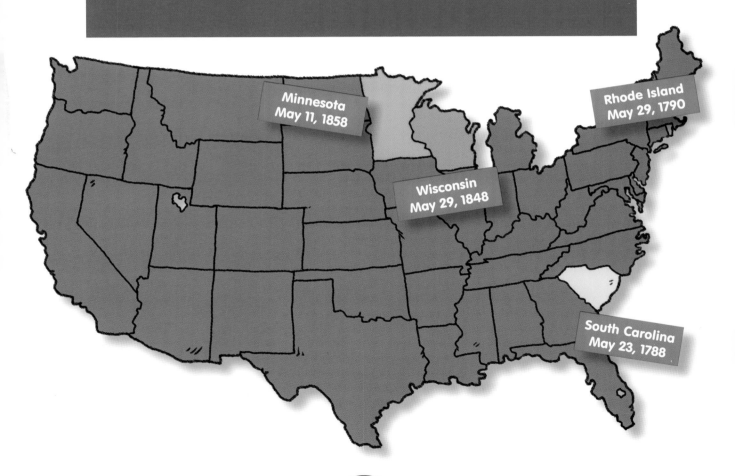

Minnesota
May 11, 1858

Rhode Island
May 29, 1790

Wisconsin
May 29, 1848

South Carolina
May 23, 1788

FAMOUS MAY BIRTHDAYS

May 2

David Beckham
Born in England, he became a world soccer star in Spain and the U.S.

May 8

President Harry Truman
Truman took over in 1945 after the death of President Franklin D. Roosevelt.

May 12

Tony Hawk
When he was a kid, the greatest skateboarder ever had a ramp in his backyard!

May 14

George Lucas

Thank this movie man for all the Star Wars and Indiana Jones movies!

May 27

Wild Bill Hickok

Wild Bill Hickok was a gunfighter, marshal, and showman in the Old West. He was born in 1837.

May 29

President John F. Kennedy

In 1960, he became the youngest person to be elected president.

May 31

Walt Whitman

This American poet's most famous work was called *Leaves of Grass*.

GLOSSARY

colony (KOL-uh-nee) A colony is an area of land that is ruled by another country.

foster children (FOSS-ter CHIL-dren) Children who are looked after by non-family members.

Maypole (MAY-pohl) A tall pole around which people dance and tie ribbons.

INDEX